The Parson and His Cemetery

Parson Wornum and his wife Jenny ride
into Sunland and into the hearts
of an entire community.

**The Early History of Sunland, California
Volume 3**

ML Tiernan

The Parson and His Cemetery

www.maryleetiernan.com
Second printing April 1, 2015
10 9 8 7 6 5 4 3 2

ISBN 978-0983067221 (Paperback)

©1999 ©2010 Mary Lee Tiernan. All rights reserved. No portion of this product may be photographed, scanned, translated, reproduced, copied, or reduced to any tangible or electronic medium or machine-readable form, without the prior written consent of Mary Lee Tiernan.

Photographs on cover courtesy of Bolton Hall Museum, Tujunga, California.
Quote on cover is the title of an old hymn.

Contents

The Parson Arrives 5

The Parson Departs 11

His Cemetery 17

Map to the Verdugo Hills Cemetery 23

Footnotes 24

Bibliography 26

The Early History of Sunland, California series 31

Author's Notes

The researcher, like a detective, examines the evidence to try to determine the real story. Unfortunately for researchers, we cannot re-examine witnesses or revisit scenes because in most cases, they have long since disappeared. So we sort through the conflicting data to find the most reliable and logical explanations. I have done my best to follow the clues and weave as authentic a story as possible.

My thanks to the staff at Bolton Hall Museum, Tujunga, California, for their assistance with this project.

The Parson Arrives

Parson Wornum and Aunt Jenny won the hearts
of an entire community.
Photo courtesy of Bolton Hall Museum.

Restless sleepers turned on their cots in the hot night air. Being outside under the stars, instead of inside hot stuffy houses, eased the difficulty of sleeping in the oppressive summer heat only slightly. Many a head was lifted from a pillow at the faint but distinct sound of horses' hooves clopping down the dirt road. Could that be…? Then a strong, familiar voice reverberated across the valley singing the old hymn "Lord, I'm Coming Home—Never More to Roam."[1] Lips curved into smiles. Only one person broke out in song that way as he drove over the ridge on Watson's Hill, the summit on Roscoe Blvd. before the road dipped down into Sunland. Once again the beloved Parson and Aunt Jenny had returned home safely.

Parson Wornum made the community aware of his presence, and that of his wife Jenny, from the first day he arrived in Sunland circa 1902. Seven-year-old George Tench bounded down Sherman Grove Avenue en route to Rowley's general store in the early morning on an errand for his mother. An old man camped under an oak tree called to him to come meet his horses. Intrigued, George did as the man had asked. After acquainting George with the handsome pair of horses, the old man introduced himself as Parson Wornum and asked George to get permission from his mother to go for a ride with him. That morning they covered the entire community as the Parson invited each family for a 'meeting' the following Sunday.

At age 62, Parson Wornum had begun tending to the needs of a new congregation.

After serving in the 83rd Illinois Infantry during the Civil War, James Thomas Wornum,[2] one of the oldest of fourteen children in a family noted for its robustness and singing ability, followed in his father's footsteps and set out on his career as an itinerant preacher of the Free Methodist Church. Sometime during the 1890s, he met and married the younger Jenny Brocus Wornum.[3] Together they traveled across the country in a covered wooden wagon drawn by a team of sturdy horses.

From the back of his wagon, the Parson held services

From his wagon, the Parson held services
whenever he could gather enough worshippers.
Photo courtesy of Bolton Hall Museum.

whenever he could gather enough worshippers. A large man, standing tall on his makeshift pulpit, his booming voice ringing with confidence in himself and his religion, he could put "...the fear of God in man and beast."[4] Then while Jenny played a small piano, both erupted into song, usually one of their favorite hymns: "Christ Is Walking on the Water," "We'll Never Say Goodbye in Heaven," or "Lord, I'm Coming Home—Never More to Roam." Their clear, strong voices captivated many a listener.

Looking down Commerce Avenue, Tujunga, toward Foothill Blvd.
The post office (first building on the left) was located on the
southeast corner of Commerce and Valmont.
Photo courtesy of Bolton Hall Museum.

While the Parson and Aunt Jenny continued circuit-riding and preaching the gospel at camp meetings, they adopted Monte Vista Valley as their home base. No longer would the little white church in the park stand vacant. For many years, the couple walked arm in arm to Sunday services where the Parson proclaimed the Lord's word with the fervor and love that defined him. Aunt Jenny taught Sunday school, and the children fondly recall the piece of candy she gave each one of them as they parted at the door.

The Parson held Sunday services in the little church in Sunland Park. In 1942, the abandoned building was moved to Valaho and Thousand Oaks in Tujunga where it was enlarged and remodeled to become the Open Bible Church, then the Tujunga Foursquare Church.
Photo courtesy of Bolton Hall Museum.

But keeping souls healthy was not the only reason the Parson and Aunt Jenny became beloved and welcomed figures in the neighborhood. The Parson earned respect and quite a reputation as a horse trader. Two strong, well-groomed horses pulled his wagon or carried the familiar figures on their backs. He trained the animals himself so well, and without abuse, that they responded equally to a command or the touch of a child's hand.

Although the Parson dedicated his life to religion, he didn't expect the same of others. His tolerance and willingness to treat everyone equally endeared him to believers and skeptics alike. During the week, the Parson helped his neighbors in their gardens or lent a hand building a house or digging a cesspool. "…and never a family in the valley was in trouble, be it sickness, death or taxes, but the old man was on hand with a prayer or a strong arm and a willing back, or even a persuasive tongue, if somebody had to be talked out of something."[5]

The Parson Departs

Realizing his age and the approaching end, the Parson often entreated his friend Marshall V. Hartranft to donate land for a cemetery so he could be buried in the hills he loved so much. Hartranft, who owned and developed much of the land in early Tujunga, kept promising he would, but as happens with busy men, kept putting off any official action.

On April 10, 1922, Dr. Virginia T. Smith was called in to treat a very ill Parson. Days later, so ill that he could barely speak above a whisper, the Parson said to Hartranft, "I'm almost ready for it, Marsh, have you given my cemetery?"[6] Horrified, Hartranft dashed to his office and cancelled all appointments. It is certainly a tribute to the Parson that such a high profile entrepreneur would drop all business for the day to grant his friend's last wish.

Hartranft grabbed his maps and anxiously studied them. Finally, "He selected a site of about four acres of foothills, called in his superintendent of construction and told him to take all his laborers and all his mules and throw a road around the main hill. The next day he went to see the Parson. 'I have your cemetery now, Parson, it's all ready for you. You can check it out any time you want,' he told him. The old man smiled a contented smile and Mr. Hartranft added, 'but, I tell you something Parson, if you'll just stick around for a while we'll show you the swellest funeral you ever saw.' The Parson grinned and promised to do it."[7] He died the next morning at 11:30 a.m. in his home.

The entire community paid their respects to their beloved Parson, accompanying him on his final journey up Parson's Trail to the new Verdugo Hills Cemetery. Photo courtesy of Bolton Hall Museum.

And thus Parson Wornum became the first to be buried in Tujunga's Verdugo Hills Cemetery, also referred to as The Hills of Peace Cemetery, at the north end of

Pinyon Street in Tujunga. The Parson could not have asked for a more breathtaking spot, high in the hills, facing the setting sun, with a magnificent vista of the valley below.

His funeral reflected the community's love for their Parson. Thinking he would be uncomfortable in a fancy automobile, neighbors drove his body in his old wagon, pulled by his beloved horses, to the foot of the hill. From there they bore the coffin a quarter of a mile up the rough winding path, now called Parson's Trail, on their shoulders.

The Parson's old wagon and his faithful horses bore the Parson to the base of Parson's Trail. Photo courtesy of Bolton Hall Museum.

For three hours on that Saturday morning, mourners climbed, following their Parson to the summit and singing his favorite hymns. Even his old saddle horses, heads lowered almost to the ground, slowly clumped their way behind their master. Two buglers, one stationed at the grave and the other on a distant hilltop, sounded taps. Their playing reverberated across the valley just as the Parson's voice had once done.

Because of the Parson's service during the Civil War, he was
accorded military honors by the American Legion.
Photo courtesy of Bolton Hall Museum.

John S. McGroarty, journalist for the *Los Angeles Times* who would later become a U.S. Congressman and the Poet Laureate of California, gave the Parson's eulogy. In days when religious denominations often clashed, no one thought it unusual for McGroarty, a devout Catholic, to lead the services for a Free Methodist. Respect for the Parson transcended such boundaries. His love had nourished the entire community and all called him friend.

McGroarty voiced his admiration. "…on the last Great Day … when he awakens, it shall be in no alien place, but in a spot well known of him and where he was well loved. His re-envisioned eyes shall behold again all with which he was so long familiar—the hills to which he lifted up his eyes and from which came his strength, the Mother Mountains at whose feet he prayed on bended knees and to whose high battlements he flung the challenge of his dauntless faith…"

Jenny died a year later and joined her husband on the highest knoll in the new cemetery. During the funeral service, John McGroarty envisioned the joy of them meeting again in another time and place. "I could see our strong old Parson … sitting on his horse, erect in the saddle as he used to sit when he rode about these hills and valleys … And beside him was another horse, waiting with an empty saddle … when the jasper gate swung open, the old Parson reached down and helped Aunt Jenny up to the waiting saddle and they galloped away…"[9]

Familiar figures on horseback ride down
Michigan Avenue (Foothill Blvd.)
Photo Courtesy of Bolton Hall Museum.

His Cemetery

Respect for the Parson and his burial place waned over the years. Drinking parties layered the cemetery with beer cans that rusted with age. Vandals pushed over gravestones, pulled off bronze and wooden markers, and even broke into the mausoleum, built in later years, to pull out bodies and scatter ashes. Weeds thrived, choking pathways and obscuring markers.

By the 1970s, the abhorrent conditions of the cemetery prompted numerous complaints. The State Cemetery Board of Directors met in February of 1971 with owners Reverend Kenton Beshore and his wife Lois Anderson about draining and erosion problems. Although the Beshores assured the Board that preliminary work had already begun for correcting the problems, by April the Beshores had to be issued an Order to Comply by the Department of Building and Safety of the City of Los Angeles to insist that they fix the grading problems.

For the next several years, newspaper headlines screamed about the plight of the cemetery, and about the

District Attorney's and State Cemetery Board's probes into the problems there. Questions arose about the misuse of endowment funds and false statements in contracts with clients. Poorly-kept records prevented clear identification of burial sites. The stench of decay seeped from unsealed mausoleum vaults. Inspections of the cemetery revealed 130 unplaced headstones and cremated remains of seven people dumped on a trash pile behind an A-frame work shed. And what did all the 'sound and fury' accomplish? The grading and erosion problems remained—sure ingredients for a catastrophe in an area with a history of periodic heavy floods.

Heavy rains tore open graves and sent corpses tumbling down the hillside.
Photo from The Record-Ledger, February 16, 1978.

And sure enough, nature supplied the final assault when heavy rains soaked the land in 1978. A little after midnight on February 9th, thunderous reverberations awoke neighbors. Some said it sounded like an earthquake; others like a train racing down Parson's Trail. A large chunk of the ground broke loose, creating a landslide that sent rocks and debris crashing down the hillside. The force of the tumbling wreckage tore open graves. In the morning, horrified homeowners found 30 bodies strewn among the refuse in their yards.[10]

A Tujunga resident stares at the leg of a corpse that washed down into her yard. Photo from the Glendale NewsPress, February 10, 1978.

City taxpayers paid a hefty $50,000 bill for emergency work after the flood. Now a public health hazard, the cemetery could no longer be ignored. Obviously, the bodies that washed down the hillside had to be re-casketed and re-interred. But the slide also exposed other graves through which lizards and other rodents darted about. Workers exhumed additional bodies to relocate them on safer ground.[11] Debris that included pieces of concrete liners and rotting wood caskets had to be cleared from roads and the hillside. And still the erosion problem needed to be solved.

In May 1980, the Beshores resigned as managers, but apparently their Institute of Christian Research remained owners.[12] The Beshores transferred reins to caretaker Bonnie Mason, who disappeared a year or so later. Without anyone on the premises, the City of Los Angeles stepped in several times in the early 1980s to clear hazardous brush and threatened to file a lawsuit against the Beshores at the Institute for unpaid bills.

Finally in December 1984, the court granted the State Cemetery Board conservatorship of the cemetery and management of the endowment funds. Unfortunately, the change did not make a big difference. In 1994, state cemetery officials voted to evict Frank Gatti, caretaker since 1988. Gatti's use of the run-down commercial A-frame 'work shed' as a home for his wife and seven children violated City codes. He also failed to pay the utility bills. After that, the water supply was shut off.

Years of neglect and human indifference have destroyed the final resting place of more than 3,000 people. As of 1999, little was being done to restore the cemetery or to provide basic maintenance. Thanks to the diligence of The Friends of the Hills of Peace Cemetery, some records now exist as to who is buried in the cemetery, but not always where. The removal of grave markers, the erosion and shifting of the earth, the mass reburials, and the negligence of caretakers have made it impossible to identify many individual gravesites.

Residents clean up the grisly devastation on the corner of Parson's Trail and Pinyon Street. Photo from The Record-Ledger, March 6, 1978.

And what about the beloved Parson? "The Parson's grave remained secure atop his rocky knoll, safe and sound on 'Higher Ground'."[13] In one sense, this is true. The first burial sites atop a small hill were not affected by the landslides, and thus, the graves remain undisturbed by the rains. But the exact location of the Parson is unknown. Vandals removed or destroyed the monument marking his grave. The Parson's original wood grave marker, rescued from destruction in the past, now reposes in Bolton Hall Museum.

#####

Route to the Verdugo Hills Cemetery

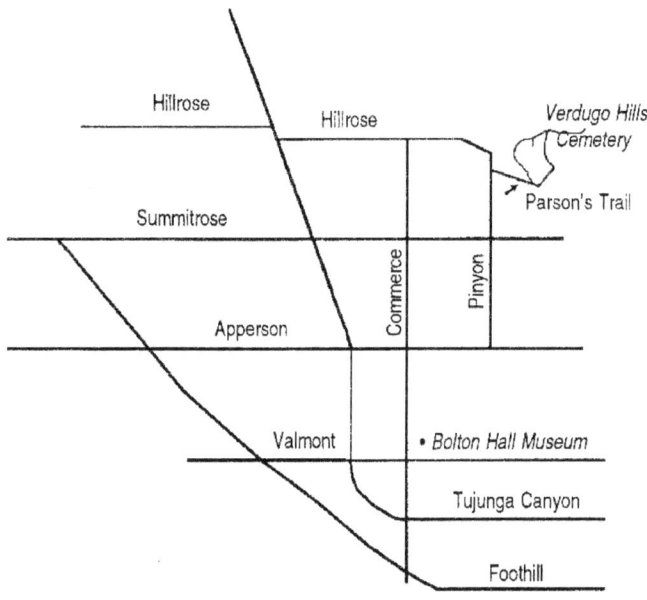

Footnotes

[1] The natural acoustics in the valley allowed sound to carry for miles. Buildings later absorbed much of the sound.

[2] James Thomas Wornum: born August 1, 1839 – died April 19, 1922.

[3] Jenny Brocus Wornum: born 1855 – died November 15, 1923. Sources show three different spellings of Jenny's maiden name: Brocos, Brocus, Brocous. Brocus if used in this document because it is the spelling used in correspondence sent by a relative to Bolton Hall Museum.

[4] Carson, Viola L., "Lord, I'm Coming Home—Never More to Roam," March 31, 1978, p. 2.

[5] Hatch, Mabel, "Horsetrading Parson Finally Got Cemetery," *The Record-Ledger, Historical & Progress Edition*, May 21, 1953, Section B, p. 5.

[6] Ibid., p. 5.

[7] Ibid., p. 5.

[8] "Parson Laid to Rest in Hills," *The Los Angeles Times*, April 24, 1922, Part II.

[9] "Pioneers Go to Their Reward," *The Record-Ledger*, Thursday, November 1, 1923.

[10] "Corpses Among Debris," *The Record-Ledger*, Saturday, March 11, 1978.

[11] Accounts differ on the actual number of bodies that needed to be relocated. One newspaper account claims 42; cemetery records indicate the number may be higher.

[12] Some documents list the Institute of Christian Research as owners, others the Hills of Peace (Cemetery). The City of Los Angeles letter threatening the lawsuit is addressed to both. Apparently the Hills of Peace is a DBA (Doing Business As) for the Institute.

[13] Carlson, Viola L. "Lord, I'm Coming Home—Never More to Roam," March 31, 1978, p. 6.

Bibliography

"Administer Suspends V.H. Cemetery Burials." *The Record-Ledger*, September 24, 1975.

"Bodies of Pioneers Rest on Hilltop." Clippings file, Bolton Hall Museum.

Bogert, John M. "Legislators Look at Cemeteries." *Glendale NewsPress*, August 14, 1976.

Carlson Viola L. "Lord, I'm Coming Home—Never More to Roam." (Essay) March 31, 1978.

Cemetery Board, State of California. Correspondence from the files of The Friends of the Hills of Peace Cemetery.

"Cemetery Directors Fix Prices." *The Record-Ledger*, February 8, 1923.

"Church Transformation." *The Record-Ledger*, Thursday, May 21, 1953.

City of Los Angeles, California. Correspondence from the files of The Friends of the Hills of Peace Cemetery.

Colville, Lucy. "Verdugo Hills Cemetery—No Peace for the Dead." *The Record-Ledger*, Thursday, April 12, 1973.

"Corpses Await Reburial." *The Record-Ledger*, Thursday, February 16, 1978.

"Corpses Among Debris." *The Record-Ledger*, February 11, 1978.

Crowell, T. Michael. "Grisly Aftermath of Flood: Cemetery Bodies Unearthed." *Glendale NewsPress*, Saturday, February 11, 1978.

Department of Building and Safety, City of Los Angeles. Correspondence from the files of The Friends of the Hills of Peace Cemetery.

"Directors Inspect Cemetery Ground." *The Record-Ledger*, January 28, 1923.

"Directors Tackle Cemetery Plans." *The Record-Ledger*, January 11, 1923.

"Foothill Flood Evacuation." *Glendale NewsPress*, Friday, February 10, 1978.

Freidman, Robert A. "Old Parson's Cemetery Is Given New Life." *The Star (Glendale NewsPress)*. September 4, 1968.

Hatch, Mabel. "Hills of Peace Restoration Is Urged by Mabel Hatch." *The Record-Ledger*, Thursday, June 9, 1955.

Hatch, Mabel. "Horsetrading Parson Finally Got Cemetery." *The Record-Ledger, Historical & Progress Edition*, May 21, 1953, Section B, p. 5.

Herrera, Arlene. Report of the Verdugo Hills Cemetery. 1955.

Hitt, Marlene. "Beloved Sunland Preacher Given a Memorable Send-off." *The Leader*, March 21, 1998.

James T. Wornum. California State Board of Health: Standard Certificate of Death. April 24, 1922.

Little Landers Historical Society. Docent Handbook. Bolton Hall Museum.

Lubas, Ken. "Deluge Sweeps 30 Bodies from Graves into Yards." *The Los Angeles Times*, Saturday, February 11, 1978.

Martinez, Al. "3 Die, 10 Sought, 30 Bodies Washed from Cemetery." *The Los Angeles Times*, Friday, February 10, 1978.

McKee, Bob. "Cemetery Probe Seeks Endowment Accounting." *The Ledger*, Thursday, August 26, 1976.

McKee, Bob. "Tujunga Cemetery Condition Probed." *The Ledger*, Thursday, August 11, 1976.

Nichols, Roberta. "6 Proposals Drawn to Aid Verdugo Hills Cemetery." *The Los Angeles Times*, Sunday, February 19, 1984.

Noguchi, Thomas T. *Coroner*. New York, NY: Simon & Schuster. 1983.

"Old Parson Packed Church in Wagon to Bring Religion to Little Landers." Clippings file, Bolton Hall Museum.

Olson, Jennifer. "Accusations Surface in Verdugo Cemetery Affairs." *The Record-Ledger,* March 24, 1977.

Parcher, Carroll. "Snow Sports More Like Self Torture." *The Leader,* Wednesday, February 22, 1984.

"Parson Laid to Rest in Hills." Clippings file, Bolton Hall Museum.

"Parson Laid to Rest in Hills." *The Los Angeles Times*, April 24, 1922. Part II.

"Parson of the Green Verdugo Hills." Clippings file. Bolton Hall Museum.

"Parson Told on Deathbed that Cemetery Was Ready for Him." *The Record-Ledger*, May 21, 1953.

"Parson's Family Visits Cemetery." *The Record-Ledger*, Monday, March 6, 1978.

"Pick Out Your Lot in the Tujunga Cemetery Friday." *The Record-Ledger*, Thursday, December 4, 1924.

"Pioneers Go to Their Reward." *The Record-Ledger*, Thursday, November 1, 1923.

"Plan Improvements at Hills of Peace." *The Record-Ledger*, July 23, 1959.

Pottage, Mike. "DA Investigators Probe Verdugo Hills Cemetery." *The Ledger*, Thursday, August 21, 1976.

Quinn, James, "Criminal Action May Be Filed in Cemetery Case." *The Los Angeles Times*, April 13, 1977.

Records of the Hills of Peace Cemetery: Compiled June 1993. Bolton Hall Museum.

"Reincarnation of Church." *The Record-Ledger*, Thursday, May 21, 1953.

Schell, A. Elizabeth. Letter to Mary Lou Pozzo. August 1996.

Schubert, Mary. "Cemetery Officials to Evict Caretaker." *Daily News*, August 2, 1994.

Schubert, Mary. "State Checking on Tujunga Cemetery." *Daily News*, July 2, 1994.

Shaffer, Gina. "Vandals, Floods Disturb Hillside Cemetery's Rest." *Daily News*, Sunday, April 19, 1987.

"Start Cemetery As Resting Place for Pioneers." *The Record-Ledger*, 1938.

Tench, George. Personal interview by Viola Carlson. April 15, 1983.

"Tujunga Cemetery Ass'n Needs Development Funds." *The Record-Ledger*, Thursday, July 26, 1956.

"Uneasy Peace." *The Los Angeles Times*, July 27, 1978.

The Early History of Sunland, California

8 Volume Series
Also available as ebooks

Vol. 1 *Hotels for the Hopeful* Land promoters of the 1880s promised a perfect life of health, wealth, and pleasure. Although their promises fell short of reality, the village did grow and prosper in the hands of farmers.

Vol. 2 *The Roscoe Robbers and the Sensational Train Robbery of 1894* Two robbers posed as passengers to flag down the train. When the engineer recognized danger, he opened the throttle and sped past. The bandits threw the spur switch, and the train careened full speed off the tracks.

Vol. 3 *The Parson and His Cemetery* Parson Wornum was so loved that when he died, the whole village attended his funeral. Years of neglect of his cemetery spelled disaster in 1978 when heavy rains tore open graves and washed bodies down the hillside.

Vol. 4 *From Crackers to Coal Oil* When a student pulled out his gun and laid it on his desk, the tiny one-room school found itself needing a new teacher. That brought Virginia Newcomb, a romance, and a new family that helped to develop the town, leaving behind a detailed account of pioneer life in a small village.

Vol. 5 *He Never Came Home* Joe Ardizzone, a local grape-grower, doubled as a hit-man for the Mafia. During Prohibition, Joe's bootlegging activities caught him in the middle of in-house quarreling. In 1931, he left on a short trip and disappeared into the pages of history.

Vol. 6 *Lancasters Lake* When Edgar Lancaster dredged the swamp on his land, he created a lake which became a treasured landmark. For 25 years, visitors flocked to its cool shores, and Hollywood used the lake as a set location for some of its early movies.

Vol. 7 *Living in Big Tujunga Canyon* Early settlers, like the Johnson family, found their way into the canyon, a dense woodland bristling with wildlife. 50 years later, the Webber family faced the wrath of the river now winding down a denuded mountainside.

Vol. 8 *From Whence They Came* The Land Boom of the 1880s brought immigrants from around the world. Two generations of Blumfields survived the difficulties of farming and water shortages through industry and imagination.

www.ingramcontent.com/pod-product-compliance
Lightning Source LLC
Chambersburg PA
CBHW061349040426
42444CB00011B/3153